FAKER

How to live for real when you're
tempted to fake it

Nicholas T. McDonald

Faker: How to live for real when you're tempted to fake it
© Nicholas T. McDonald/The Good Book Company 2015

Reprinted 2016

Published by
The Good Book Company
Tel (UK): 0333 123 0880
International: +44 (0) 208 942 0880
Email: info@thegoodbook.com

Websites:
North America: www.thegoodbook.com
UK: www.thegoodbook.co.uk
Australia: www.thegoodbook.com.au
New Zealand: www.thegoodbook.co.nz

Unless indicated, all Scripture references are taken from the HOLY BIBLE, NEW INTERNATIONAL VERSION. Copyright © 1973, 1978, 1984, 2011 by Biblica, Inc.® Used by permission.

ISBN: 9781909919433

Printed in the UK

Design and illustration by André Parker

Contents

Introduction

Have you ever felt like a *faker*?

I have.

I've felt like no one in the world knew who I was. I've felt like I had to be someone I'm not. I've felt like, no matter who I was, no one would care.

I've felt alone. I've felt like I was living with a mask. And I've seen others wearing masks, too. Maybe you've looked around your work or school and thought: "What are we all doing? Why are we all trying to impress each other? Why can't anyone accept me for who I am?"

If you feel that way, you're not alone. This book is, in a lot of ways, about my time through high-school and college. It's about feeling like I was living on a roller coaster, panicking about everyone's opinion of me, all the time. It's about feeling like I had to live a double—no, triple—life just to keep up.

If you've ever felt any of those things, I'm with you. I want to talk with you. I want to introduce you to the journey I took that changed my life forever.

And I want to show you through a simple story Jesus told, 2,000 years ago.

If that sounds like something you want, read on.

To some who were confident of their own righteousness and looked down on everyone else, Jesus told this parable: "Two men went up to the temple to pray, one a Pharisee and the other a tax collector. The Pharisee stood by himself and prayed: 'God, I thank you that I am not like other people—robbers, evildoers, adulterers—or even like this tax collector. I fast twice a week and give a tenth of all I get.'

"But the tax collector stood at a distance. He would not even look up to heaven, but beat his breast and said, 'God, have mercy on me, a sinner.'

"I tell you that this man, rather than the other, went home justified before God. For all those who exalt themselves will be humbled, and those who humble themselves will be exalted."

Luke 18 v 9-14

Chapter One:
The problem with being a wallflower

"I'm Tony Stark. I build neat stuff, got a great girl, occasionally save the world. So why can't I sleep?"

Tony Stark, *Iron Man 3*

I only made one good impression during my first year of school in Toledo, and that was in Ronny B's gut. He called me a name, so I punched him. After that, my family moved three hours north to a magical land called Michigan. There, I hoped to make a name for myself. In fact, I had a name in mind: "Crazy Nick", as in: "Who, him? Oh yeah, that's Nick McDonald, but we call him CRAZY Nick."

So before Scott, my new Michigan neighbor, arrived on the doorstep, I threw myself upside-down in a toy-box. It was my simple way of saying: "I'm crazy. See?" But after an hour, the plastic Ninja Turtle sword prodding my forehead felt like it was leaving a permanent mark. So I stood up, and Scott walked in, staring at me like I was the purple-faced

9

mop-headed Muppet I was. I did look crazy—the kind of crazy that makes people say: "I wonder if he takes his meds—let's lock our front doors."

A year later, I decided to quit the "Crazy Nick" campaign for a nickname. I went with "Butterball," not knowing it was a term for "well-fed" fellows like me… I just knew it was my favorite brand of turkey.

The kids on the playground laughed. A few years later, I got the joke.

From my first years in school, I had instinctively known the truth about life: **If I wanted to get ahead, I had to be a *faker*.** The only difference was, back then, I wasn't good at it.

The ease of faking it

In our social-media-saturated world, it's easy to be fake. We hand-select what we want people to know about us. For example, I have yet to post *Facebook* photos of me blowing my nose, sitting on the toilet, or glaring at *YouTube* videos of cat birthday parties.

In fact, I've never posted a status about what I'm actually doing: looking at *Facebook*. What would I even say? "Totes staring at other people's lives right now. SUPER jelly. Spending the weekend alone. LOL." Here are things I'd rather have posted about me:

O Great jokes I made

O Profound quotes I found

O Fun times with besties

It's the same with *Instagram*, *Twitter*, *Tumblr*, etc. I've never instagrammed a "C" on a math test. As far as I remember, I've never tweeted: "I just told a joke. No one laughed." Looking at my life through

social-media lenses, you'd think I had it all. And that's exactly what I want you to think.

But sometimes I wonder: **"What would people think if they really knew me?"**

The pressure of faking it

I grew up in the church, which is what you might call a faker breeding ground. There, I learned to slick my hair to the side and regurgitate answers to Bible questions. It's easier than you might think:

"Kids, what has four wheels, drives down the highway, and blares a siren during emergencies?"

"JESUS!"

"No, but YOUNG MAN, YOU HAVE A HEART FOR THE LORD."

The music director at my church dubbed me "Smiling Nick," because that's all I ever did. I showed up. I smiled. I left.

My friends called me "Frank Rizzo." It was the name I used to make prank calls. Frank made sex jokes, racial jokes, cussing jokes, smoking jokes, drinking jokes, and religion jokes. I thought it was okay to be "Frank Rizzo," because he was imaginary. Sort of.

But halfway through high school, I realized Frank Rizzo was getting more attention than I was. I was jealous. So, I started asking: "What would Frank do?" I snuck into movies, looked at raunchy pictures,

bought expensive clothes, and pulled pranks on kids who weren't like me.

Life was going swimmingly for Frank Rizzo. But it seemed like life wasn't going well for me.

At night, I'd lay on my bed, wondering: What if I couldn't be funny anymore? Or worse, what if I had to go on being funny forever? Or what if, by some freak accident, the world of Frank Nick and Smiling Nick collided and formed a black hole in my perfectly crafted universe, thus swallowing me whole along with the rest of humankind as we know it, plummeting us into an eternal abyss of confusion and mass chaos from which there was no recovery? What THEN, I ask you?

Maybe you feel the same way. Maybe you wonder to yourself:

"What if I stop getting straight A's?"

"What if, with two minutes left in the game, I flop?"

"What if they see me without my makeup?"

"What if the people at church find out?"

Maybe you feel like giving up. Maybe you just feel tired.

The confusion of faking it

In my last two years of high-school, the pressure of being "Frank" overwhelmed me. I couldn't keep track of the stories I made up. My punch-lines got old. Before seeing friends, I felt like puking.

So, I quit.

I stopped making jokes. I became a wallflower. People asked me what was wrong with me, and I thought: "What's wrong with me? I don't know who I am." **I had been a human chameleon so long, I forgot what color I was.**

I didn't want to be a faker, but I didn't know what else to be. I was confused. I was alone.

So, I went back to my roots: I got religion.

Coping with faking it

Religion, as I've said, is a pretty easy gig. I knew how to work the system. I went on mission trips. I served at camps. I read books. I bought Christian T-shirts. I listened to Christian music. I could've gone pro, if that was a thing. Sure, Jesus loved everybody. But he actually *liked* me!

Church people applauded me. My unchurched friends respected me. Home-school moms swooned. My pastor called me "Saint Nick." I thought I'd finally hit my stride—maybe this Jesus thing wasn't so bad after all.

But as time wore on, I began to feel something was missing. I didn't understand: I was doing all the right things. I was following all the rules. So why did I still feel so… fake? Why did I still go home and ask the same questions: "What if people really knew me? What would they think? What if people at church find out about my flaws?"

And then it hit me. The reason I felt fake being religious Nick was simple: I *wasn't* religious Nick.

Religion, for me, was a springboard to what I really wanted: applause, attractiveness, attention… for me. You might even say **religious Nick was Frank Nick with plastic surgery**. The only difference was, now people thought I loved Jesus.

I didn't. I didn't love anyone else, either. Maybe I should say it this way: I *couldn't*. It's pretty tough to love God or anyone when you're afraid they won't approve of you. And at the time, I was terrified.

I like the way Tony Stark put it at the beginning of the chapter, don't you? "I'm Tony Stark. I build neat stuff, got a great girl, occasionally save the world. So why can't I sleep?" On the surface, Stark is successful—he has everything. But he's haunted.

Throughout the movie, when things get tough, Stark turns to the one thing he can control: his mask, the Iron Man suit. And while it provides temporary comfort, slowly it begins to take over and destroy everything around him. He can't function without his mask.

I wonder if that's not so different from what you and I do, every day; we constantly pull away from who we are, because we're riddled with fear and personal guilt. We turn, again and again, to whatever "mask" we've created for ourselves—the Jokester, the Smart Kid, the Athlete, the Fashionista. Even being a social outcast can become a mask—we start doing everything to "not be like the sell-outs," and so we stop being ourselves.

And we do it all because, deep down, we're afraid. What if the mask comes off? What if people knew what I know about me? What if the people who hate me are right, and the people who love me are wrong? What then?

And so **we interact with the world at a distance**; we're in a conversation with friends, but we keep slipping back to our iPhone. Why? We're afraid.

We've accumulated a massive list of friends and followers, but few have had dinner at our house. Why? We're afraid.

We'd rather calculate our words through text than talk

face to face. Why? Because you, me, all of us—we're terrified that people will see us.

And so life is an endless game of peekaboo.

But what if I told you there was a way out?

A story for fakers

In AD 30, on the barren outskirts of Jerusalem, a man named Jesus told a story.

Some people were angry about this story, because it was part of Jesus' campaign to strip us—all of us—of our masks. Those people killed him.

Other people heard, and their hearts burned within them. That fire extended outward, charring away their masks, and spreading into an explosive, authentic community that turned the world upside down (Acts 17 v 6).

I am praying for you, as I write. I am praying you would be free from your mask. I am praying you would find that community.

I am praying you would **turn the world upside down**.

Chapter Two:
The faker roller coaster

TODAY'S TEST:
1) GIRLS
2) SPAM

To some who were confident of their own righteousness and looked down on everyone else, Jesus told this parable...
Luke 18 v 9

"The monsters are my medicine. They heal me, physically and emotionally, every night at the show ... I worship little monsters. They're my religion." Lady Gaga[1]

There's another danger of faking. It's not a danger for us—it's a danger for others. I've seen it before.

I was 10 years old, and her name was Rachel P. She had beautiful black hair, a nice smile, and a sense of humor. Her most attractive feature, however, was her willingness to speak to me.

I didn't know much about girls, except:

1. They conducted all key business in support groups which congregated in the girl's restroom.

2. I knew as much about this business as the ingredients in a can of Spam. Therefore...

3. I was clueless about talking to Rachel P.

So, when we found a topic of conversation—Sarah and Johnny—I clung on for dear life.

Sarah and Johnny were what you might call... Freaks. Geeks. Dorks. Outsiders. Losers. Which meant that the material they produced for Rachel and me was pure gold.

For weeks, Rachel and I swapped stories about Sarah and Johnny's awkwardness. It felt good to have an attractive girl tell me I wasn't like them. They were the people we made fun of. I was the funny one.

Then came Valentine's Day, 1997. I was going to prove to Rachel that I was cool. I was going to write a love letter. So I gathered my supplies: a pack of those Valentine's sweet-hearts that taste like mildly strawberry-tainted chalk, a plastic bag, paper and a pen.

"Dear Sarah," my letter read. "You are SOOOOOOO hot. Love, Johnny." Rachel snickered.

"Are you really going to do it?" she asked.

"Watch me," I said. During lunch, I slipped the bag into Sarah's cubby. I fidgeted all afternoon, not entirely sure when the punch line would come. At 2:30pm, my sweet, southern teacher, Mrs. S, gathered the class together for a special announcement. She pulled a familiar crumpled bag from her pocket.

"Whoever did this," said Mrs. S, holding up my hilarious prank, "is **lower than a snake's belly**." No one laughed.

And then it hit me: Sarah and Johnny weren't just jokes. They were people.

And that made Mrs. S's calculations exactly correct: I was lower than a snake's belly, because I thought I was better than them.

What Jesus hates

Being a faker is ugly. Not only does it cause us to live on an emotional roller-coaster, it also causes us to **look down on others when their masks aren't as pretty as ours**.

And that ticks Jesus off. We hear it in the introduction to Jesus' story (or parable):

> *To some who were confident of their own righteousness and looked down on everyone else, Jesus told this parable...*
>
> *Luke 18 v 9*

What does it mean to look down on others? It means:

O excluding Sarah and Johnny from conversations.

O turning a blind eye when people make fun of Sarah and Johnny.

O talking about Sarah and Johnny on the bus.

O writing a fake love letter from Johnny to Sarah.

Looking down on others is: *looking at Sarah and Johnny and seeing something less valuable than me*.

You can see why this makes Jesus angry. **What would the world be like if no one looked down on anyone else?** No mean pranks. No gossip. No exclusion. No nasty texts. No pornography. No bullying. No commiserating about terrible teachers.

And also, no sex slaves. No terrorists. No rich countries exploiting poor countries. No African apartheid. No Nazis killing Jews.

See, **the seeds of gossip and mass-murder are sown in the same moment**—one person looks at another and says: "Because of my race, my religion, my education, my clothes, my family, my friends… I'm better."

The roller coaster of self-righteousness

Where does this sense of "betterness" come from? Notice how Luke ties these two things together in his introduction:

To some who were confident of their own righteousness and looked down on everyone else, Jesus told this parable…

Luke 18 v 9

1. Trusting in our own righteousness, *and...*

2. Looking down on others.

Trusting in our own righteousness means: to believe that we are good, we're worthy of love, we've "got it right"—according to us. See, before I pranked Sarah and Johnny, I had to make a decision: "Being good, for me, means being liked by Rachel P."

What does being "good" mean to you?

O That guy realizing you're a princess.

O Your teacher commending you for grades.

- O That group wanting you to sit with them at lunch.

- O Walking into church and receiving a pat on the back.

- O People ogling at your beach body.

- O Crowds "oohing" and "aahing" as you make the winning shot.

The problem with these things is this:

1. We achieve it, and we feel better than others—which Jesus hates, *or...*

2. We don't achieve it, and **we feel as small as a shriveled pistachio**.

Either way, we're living in constant fear: fear we won't measure up. Fear we can't repeat our performance. Fear they'll change their mind.

Fear we'll be stripped of our mask, and everyone will see us stark naked.

Three kinds of fear

Remember in the last chapter how we said fear is what leads to faking? Jesus shows us in this parable where that fear comes from. It comes from us deciding what will make us good, right and worthy of love: trusting in ourselves that we are righteous.

In my own life, I've seen this happen in three ways:

1. **"They will like me when..." syndrome.** Yes, there was Rachel P. There were also the skaters I tried to fit in with. The jocks I tried to hang out with. The nerds I tried to keep up with. I even tried the cross-country kids. Later, it was the boss I wanted to impress. Parents I wanted to please. My wife and kids I wanted to look up to me. In every case, everything I did was measured by: "Will they like this?" And the *faker roller coaster* continued.

2. **"I will like me when…" syndrome.** I've been here many times: I will like me when I publish a book. When I get good grades. When I have more money. When I become a professional hockey player. (Yes, I thought that would happen—I'm not sure exactly why.) On the list goes: things I had to achieve before I was likeable. But all of these things send me down the faker roller coaster—when I do well, I look down on others; when I don't, I feel terrible.

3. **"God will like me when…" syndrome.** This is a tricky one, because it sounds good. God will like me when I stop looking at porn. When I have my anger under control. When I go to church. When I read my Bible. When I quit my addictions. When I achieve nirvana (if I'm a Buddhist), or keep Adhan (if I'm a Muslim), or become one with the universe. The problem with this approach is this: it's self-righteousness in disguise. Think about it: did GOD ever say he would like you when you achieve these things? Or, was that you, or some other mere human? People who have this problem often say things like: "I know God forgives me, but I just can't forgive myself." And really, that makes US God, doesn't it?

Of course, achieving these things never really satisfies. It's why Lady Gaga, when she had over 41 million twitter followers, still needed attention like she needed medicine: "The monsters (Gaga fans) are my medicine," she confessed in an interview. "They heal me, physically and emotionally, every night at the show … I worship little monsters. They're my religion."

Gaga had found her self-righteousness: she was loved by millions. But she needed more. That's because fame

will never quench our thirst for true "rightness." Neither will money, or success, or popularity, or approval from our religious leaders.

Self-righteousness is never *satisfying* righteousness.

The godless solution

So, what is the solution? The solution—let me put my cards on the table—starts with God. So if you don't believe in God, you could stop reading.

But before you do, I'd like to ask you a question. Do you believe, like Jesus, that the world would be a better place if no one said: "I'm better"? If you do, let me ask you something else: *why?*

Think about it: if there is no God, then life is all about "survival of the fittest." And if that's true... don't I have a right to look down on other people? Isn't terrorism just one group surviving over another? What about surgical experiments on the disabled? What about powerful countries oppressing weaker countries? Isn't it all just one group "winning" and another group "losing"?

That probably makes you uncomfortable. I know it does me. That's because God has given us a gift—**deep down, each of us knows that there's something to live for beyond "survival."** We know, deep down, that everyone is infinitely valuable. It's why you don't attend funerals and say: "Progress." It's why you don't see mangled bodies and say: "Natural." It's why you don't look at African-American slavery and say: "They lost. Oh, well."

You know, deep down, that we're not just survivors. We're equals— black, white, rich, poor, smart, dull—all of us. And the reason why we're equals is this: we're created equal, and equally valuable, in the image of God.

The religious solution

If you're coming from another religious perspective, let me ask you something: is your religion making you real, or fake? See, every religion but Christianity (true Christianity, which comes from the Bible) offers a list of do's and don'ts—"God (or gods, or the universe) will like me when…". But that only furthers our fakeness, doesn't it? When we obey  the rules, we look down on others. Even when we're "tolerant," we look down on people who aren't. When we can't obey, we're riddled with guilt, and we run from God and others.

The Bible offers a different solution. The Bible says the problem with self-righteousness is this: the instant we say: "I'll be good/right/worthy of love according to me," is the instant we say: *"I am the king and judge over my own life."*

This is why, according to Scripture, simply looking in the mirror and saying "I'm great" isn't going to work. We don't need more of our opinion—we need less of it! What we need is a new King and Judge—one who is overwhelming, and beautiful, and dangerous, and good. **We need a God so big that he makes our opinions,**

and the opinions of others, irrelevant. We need a God who dethrones us.

But in order to have that, we'll need to enter the most dangerous place on earth.

That's exactly where our story continues.

Chapter Three:
Dangerously good

Two men went up to the temple to pray, one a Pharisee and the other a tax collector.   *Luke 18 v 10*

"Deep down, everyone is just faking it until they figure it out."
April Ludgate, NBC's *Parks and Recreation*

Have you ever been overwhelmed? I have. My college buddies and I had spent a year saving up for a trip to travel west to camp for two weeks in Yellowstone National Park. At the time, **the closest thing we'd seen to wildlife was the leftover pizza in our refrigerator**. So we were amped.

We loaded up our cars, and spent 22 hours driving, non-stop.

I remember that moment, when we saw it: blue, snow-capped mountains appeared over the horizon like ghosts. As the week went by, we saw things that took our breath away: geysers shooting 200 foot streams of water, rainbows suspended over waterfalls, packs of wolves, buffalo and mountain goats meandering in front of our car.

As the trip concluded, I started to have this strange sensation that somehow, I'd stepped into reality. Life in college had revolved around me. My dorm. My songs. My movies. My, my, my.

Out here, I was an intruder; I was a footnote; I was *small*.

And no matter what background we come from, I think we can all agree: the world doesn't really revolve around "me," does it? In fact, I know that the moments when I forget myself—the moments when I'm overwhelmed by beauty—are the moments when I feel most alive. It's like Beatrice Prior said in Veronica Roth's *Divergent*: "This is the first time I'm happy I'm so small."

When was the last time you felt small?

Hamburger flipping vs. "I Am"

If I were to ask you how you feel about God, what would be your gut reaction? Confused? Bored? Curious?

How about *overwhelmed*? I'm guessing not.

I'll be honest: sometimes I picture God like he's a hamburger-flipping employee behind the counter, nervously taking my order: *Yes, you'd like a bit of religion your way? That'll be church attendance for two weeks straight, please. Then I'll do whatever you like, honest!*

But if I'm honest, I realize—that god sounds an awful lot like me. He's the kind of god I'd make up, if I could (which means I probably did). He's certainly not a god who can kick me off my throne. No—I need a god *who doesn't need my approval* to do that. **And that's exactly who the God of the Bible is.**

The God of Scripture says: "I Am who I Am" (Exodus 3 v 14). Which means: *No matter who you'd like me to be, I am myself. There's no one and nothing like me.* When God's people began turning to other gods and doing horrible injustice to their own people, God said their central problem was this: "When you did these things and I kept silent, *you thought I was exactly like you.*" (Psalm 50 v 21, italics mine)

See, the God of the Bible is a God I wouldn't have made up. He's a God who's over me, not a god who's under my thumb. He's a God who confronts me about my claim to the throne of my life. And we find out about him in the place where Jesus' story happens: the temple. It was a place that reminded God's people of three core truths about his character: **God is the rightful, ruling and returning King of the world**.

The rightful King

First, the temple reminded God's people that he was the *rightful* King and Judge of the universe. If you could tour the temple, you'd see hundreds of symbols: stars, pomegranates, thickets of trees, flowers, water, etc. Why? Because these things reflected God's glory in creation: "He built his sanctuary like the heights, like the earth that he established forever" (Psalm 78 v 69).[1]

The message was: God created the world we love. Whether it's sex, Marvel movies, music scales, dog-slobber, crackling fires, Yellowstone park or salted caramel mochas—it was all his idea: "For since the creation of the world God's invisible qualities—his eternal power and divine nature—have been clearly seen, being understood from what has been made" (Romans 1 v 20).

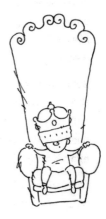

These things pointed to God's right to be King and Judge. How? Think of it this way: I like to play Legos with my son, Caleb. Sometimes, we (okay, I) try to build a monster-mega-super-duper tower that reaches the ceiling. And usually, about three-quarters of the way through, my son asks: "Can I knock it down?"

To which I reply: "Absolutely not."

To which he replies: "Why?"

To which I reply: "Because *I made it*."

To which he replies: "Humph!"

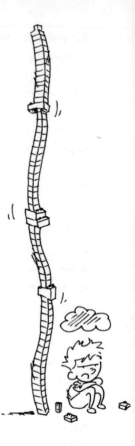

If my 4-year-old gets it, I think you probably do, too. **God made the world, which means—it's his.** "You are worthy, our Lord and God, to receive glory and honor and power, for you created all things, and by your will they were created and have their being" (Revelation 4 v 11).

For us fakers, this is incredibly powerful; because when I'm tempted to judge myself, or when I'm tempted to cherish other people's judgment of me, I can remind myself: "I don't have the right to be King and Judge. They don't have the right to be King and Judge. God, who created this world, does."

The ruling King

The second thing the temple communicated was this: God is the *ruling* King and Judge of the universe. In the center of the temple, behind a curtain, was a place called the "Most Holy Place." There, you would find all kinds of dazzling, precious stones, and two gigantic angels called "cherubim," bowing down and covering their faces, surrounded by a thick cloud veiling the presence of God.

This part of the temple was a picture of God's heavenly throne room. Specifically, the golden ark in the center of the room symbolized the place where God's throne touched earth—God's footstool. So King David says: "Listen to me, my fellow Israelites, my people. I had it in my heart to build a house as a place of rest for the ark of the covenant of the LORD, *for the footstool of our God*, and I made plans to build it." (1 Chronicles 28 v 2, italics mine)

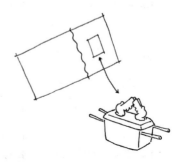

The imagery of God's heavenly throne room communicates this: **the world, at this moment, is being orchestrated by God**. The temple pictures the world like a giant tree, where the branches of God's reign spread over the earth, and the roots sink deep into everything (1 Kings 6 v 29); or a river, out of which God's life flows and sustains us (Ezekiel 47 v 1-12). (Yes, I realize I am a nerd but COME ON—that's really cool!)

This is the point: God not only has the *right* to be King—he *is* King. Again, this is great news for fakers. Whenever I'm tempted to think that my failures are devastating, or think I made myself successful, I can look to this truth: *God, the King and Judge, is truly in control. Not me. He gives, and takes away.* Whenever I'm tempted to fret about pleasing people, I can remember: "These people don't have ultimate power. God does. He controls my life, not them."

The returning King

The final thing the temple communicated was this: God is the *returning* King and Judge of the universe.

When God created the first temple, it wasn't built with bricks.
It was a garden—the Garden of Eden. There he placed two temple guardians: Adam and Eve. He told them: "Be fruitful and increase in number; fill the earth and subdue it. Rule over the fish in the sea and the birds in the sky and over every living creature that moves on the ground" (Genesis 1 v 28). In other words: *make the rest of the world like my temple.*

Why? Because the temple was the place of God's glory. As Adam and Eve acted as God's image and spread his temple, all of creation would see the beauty of God.

But Adam and Eve failed—they rebelled against the King.

So years later, God commissioned a man named Noah to fulfill his original command (Genesis 8 v 17).

But Noah failed, too.

So God did something radical. **He didn't command but instead *promised* to spread his temple-glory**, through a man named Abram (Genesis 12 v 1-3). And he would do that by dwelling with Abram's descendants, first through the tabernacle (which is like a tent); then through the temple.

That all changed with the arrival of Jesus Christ. After Jesus returned to heaven, the Jerusalem Temple was no longer the place where God's people had access to him. Instead, "through [Jesus] we ... have access to the Father" (Ephesians 2 v 18).

And for those who come to God through Jesus, God made another promise, later: "My dwelling place will be with them; I will be their God, and they will be my people. Then the nations will know

that I the LORD make Israel holy, when my sanctuary is among them forever" (Ezekiel 37 v 27-28) . Soon, God would dwell "among" his people, not in a tent or a temple, but in an entirely renovated heaven and earth (Isaiah 65 v 17). This is the Bible's ultimate vision: not a cartoon heaven where naked babies sit on clouds stroking harps—but **a real earth, filled with God's beauty**.

This last bit of truth is powerful for fakers like you and me because it means that when I'm tempted to daydream about my own fame, or beat myself up for my failures, I can say: "This story isn't about *me*. It's about God." Whenever I'm tempted to envy people who've climbed the social ladder, or look down on people who haven't, I can remind myself: "This story isn't about any of us getting glory. It's about God, and his glory."

Overwhelmed?

When we dwell on these three truths, they dethrone us—along with everyone else. It's the beginning of the path out of *Fakerville*. Before moving on, here are some Bible passages that help remind me that God is the true King and Judge of my universe. I encourage you to read through a couple before moving on, then read the rest when you've finished the book. Think of this time like pumping up a Super-Squirter gun—**the more time you spend thinking on God's bigness now, the more packed will be the punch of God's message** in the rest of the book:

O Job 38 - 41

O Isaiah 6:1-6

O Revelation 4

O Psalm 8/29/47

O Exodus 3

Done it? Good. Hopefully now you're saying: "I've got it—God is King and Judge, not me or others. But here's the thing: **How am I supposed to know what God thinks about me?**"

Great question.

In fact, it's what Jesus' story is all about.

Chapter Four:
The walking dead

Jesus told this parable: "Two men went up to the temple to pray, one a Pharisee and the other a tax collector. The Pharisee stood by himself and prayed: 'God, I thank you that I am not like other people—robbers, evildoers, adulterers—or even like this tax collector. I fast twice a week and give a tenth of all I get.'"

Luke 18 v 9-12

"The monsters that rose from the dead, they are nothing compared to the ones we carry in our hearts."

Max Brooks, *World War Z: An Oral History of the Zombie War*

Let's say a radical terrorist group called the "Bazaars" starts a chemical warfare that wipes out half your population. They behead your government leaders. They take over.

Now wherever you go, the "Bazaars" follow you. On vacation, the Bazaars stop you, rifle through your stuff, and hijack whatever they want. Once a year, your family pays taxes and the Bazaars jack half your life savings— some for the government, some for themselves.

Now imagine your get-rich-quick Great Uncle Marvin decides to join them. He revokes his family faith, and is promoted to a life of luxury: he beats on his old friends and neighbors, raids your wallet at will, and takes advantage of your mother and father.

Marvin is what you might call a scumbag.

Marvin is what people in Jesus' time called "a tax collector."

The Pharisees: a good lot

Now imagine the most devout, religious person you can think of. Let's say he's an old man named Gamaliel:

- O Gamaliel gives 10% of everything he has to his church. He even goes out into his garden to collect 10% of his produce.

- O Twice a week, Gamaliel starves himself in order to focus on God in prayer.

- O Gamaliel follows a strict *kosher* (Jewish religious) diet, and washes his whole body before every meal. (He doesn't eat bacon, and to me that is hardcore.)

- O Three times a day, Gamaliel stops whatever he's doing to go to church for prayer.

- O Gamaliel reads his Bible every day—in fact, he has the first five books of the Bible entirely memorized. That's 79,847 words (and you thought memorizing every lyric to every Taylor Swift song EVER was impressive, didn't you?).

- O Gamaliel wears a religious robe with tassels on it to remind himself to pray. It's the ancient equivalent of "I liked Jesus on Facebook—how about you?" (Yup, I've seen it.)

- O Every year, Gamaliel goes on a mission trip to teach people about his faith.

- O Gamaliel teaches Sunday School at his church every week, and spends hours translating and studying the Scriptures.

Gamaliel, in other words, is the most devout man you've ever met.

Gamaliel is what people in Jesus' time called "a Pharisee."

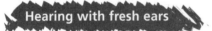

Hearing with fresh ears

Now imagine you are sitting, listening to Jesus—a devout Jewish rabbi—introduce his story: "Two men went up to the temple to pray, one a Pharisee and the other a tax collector." What do you think comes next? Keep in mind: this all takes place in the temple, the place where God shows that he is King and Judge.

I'm thinking something like: *Machine-Gun Rabbi II: Gamaliel's Revenge.*

The camera pans toward the devout Pharisee:

> *The Pharisee stood by himself and prayed: "God, I thank you that I am not like other people—robbers, evildoers, adulterers—or even like this tax collector. I fast twice a week and give a tenth of all I get."*   Luke 18 v 11-12

The Pharisee is good, and he knows it. He hasn't become like the "robbers, evildoers, adulterers" around him. He hasn't sold out like the tax collector. He is part of the resistance. He's humble about it, too—he thanks God that he's good.

But something stinks.

The incredible twist

Let me give you a little background. Jesus, a few chapters earlier, had some choice words for the Gamaliels of the world—the Pharisees:

1. **Jesus says the Pharisees care more about *looking* pure than *being* pure.** "Now then, you Pharisees clean the outside of the cup and dish, but inside you are full of greed and wickedness. You foolish people! Did not the one who made the outside make the inside also? But now as for what is inside you—be generous to the poor, and everything will be clean for you" (Luke 11 v 39-41).

2. **Jesus says the Pharisees care more about *looking* generous than *being* generous.** "Woe to you Pharisees, because you give God a tenth of your mint, rue and all other kinds of garden herbs, but you neglect justice and the love of God. You should have practiced the latter without leaving the former undone" (Luke 11 v 42).

3. **Jesus says the Pharisees care more about *looking* reverent than *being* reverent.** "Woe to you Pharisees, because you love the most important seats in the synagogues and respectful greetings in the marketplaces" (Luke 11 v 43).

4. **Jesus says the Pharisees cared more about *looking* alive than *being* alive.** "Woe to you, because you are like unmarked graves, which people walk over without knowing it" (Luke 11 v 44).

Even though the Phari-
sees had all the trappings
of goodness, the truth
was they were fakers. In
fact, one word Jesus uses
to describe Pharisees—
"hypocrites"—literally
meant to be a "masked
man" in the theater (Luke 13 v 15).[1] This is also why Jesus calls them
"unmarked graves" or "whitewashed tombs" (Matthew 23 v 27).
On the outside, they were pretty. But on the inside, they were dead,
religious zombies.

So even though the Pharisee in our story looks like a duck, and quacks
like a duck, **he doesn't smell like a duck: he smells like death**.

The Pharisee's false standard

The problem with the Pharisee wasn't that he prayed a lot, fasted,
and gave his money to the temple. These were all good things. The
problem with the Pharisee was this: the Pharisee had made himself
king and judge over his own life. That's what it means, if you'll remember, to be "self-righteous": to be good according to *me*.

And because of that, he was stepping on others to keep his throne.
Listen to his prayer: the Pharisee refers to his own goodness four
times in two sentences: "*I* thank you... *I* am not like other people...
I fast twice a week... *I* give a tenth of all *I* get."

And while at first glance this might sound nice and healthy, a closer
look shows us what this is all about: *the Pharisee is pronouncing
himself righteous in front of God, the true King.* In fact, nothing the
Pharisee lists has anything to do with God's law given to the Jewish
people. He's made up his own standard of righteousness.

The Pharisee isn't loving his neighbor as God's law requires—instead, he looks down on his neighbors, so he can feel good about himself. He doesn't love God with all his heart, soul, mind and strength, as the law says: he's using God for his own ego-grooming. He's like a terrible date: "Nice to meet you. Now let me talk about myself for an hour."

It's a bit like the Pharisee **stepped into God's throne room to build an altar to himself**.

The fault in our Pharisee

The Pharisee is a picture of who we all are: we have made ourselves king and judge over our lives—so we trample on others to keep our throne. I like how Augustus Waters said it in his letter to Hazel in John Green's *The Fault In Our Stars*:

> *Almost everyone is obsessed with leaving a mark upon the world. Bequeathing a legacy. Outlasting death. We all want to be remembered. I do, too. That's what bothers me most, is being another unremembered casualty in the ancient and inglorious war against disease. I want to leave a mark.*
>
> *But ... the marks humans leave are too often scars. You build a hideous mini-mall or start a coup or try to become a rock star and you think, "They'll remember me now," but (a) they don't remember you, and (b) all you leave behind are more scars. Your coup becomes a dictatorship. Your mini-mall becomes a lesion ...*
>
> *We are like a bunch of dogs squirting on fire hydrants.*

I love the way he puts that: **we are like dogs, leaving our mark on the world**. We want to say to every square inch of it: "I'm king. That's mine." And so, like the Pharisee, we leave scars on the lives of others. In trying to build our own kingdom, we climb over others, insult them, and look down on them, like the Pharisee with the tax collector.

Our little kingdom becomes our little dictatorship. And that's what Jesus hates.

If you're saying: "Thank you God, that I'm not like that Pharisee!" here's a question: what is your standard for being good? Is it to "Love the Lord your God with all your heart and with all your soul and with all your strength and with all your mind" (Luke 10 v 27)? I know I spend more time fantasizing about my goodness than God's goodness. I use my words to promote myself, not God—my Creator, King and Judge. Which means I've made myself king and judge, not him.

Here's another question: do you "love your neighbor as yourself" (Luke 10 v 27b)? You might think "Yes," but remember: loving people isn't the same as getting them to like you. The Pharisees, after all, loved it when people liked them. But they didn't love people. They didn't give, unless they got something back: respect, praise, popularity, money, etc.

So, are you a people-*pleaser* or a people-*lover*?

I know I spend more time getting people to like me than thinking of their good—especially

41

when it comes to people who don't catapult me up the social ladder. When people don't approve of me, or when they insult me, I quickly retreat. **I'm not interested in them—I'm interested in their admiration.**

But these attitudes are what make us fakers in the first place. When we try to usurp God's throne, we need to do whatever it takes to win the respect of others; we'll fit whatever mold they so choose. And we end up ignoring God's true standards: love of him and others.

That—and I mean this in the most literal way imaginable—is a deadly place to be.

Which is what makes the tax collector's prayer brilliant…

Chapter Five:
Looking under the hood

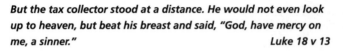

But the tax collector stood at a distance. He would not even look up to heaven, but beat his breast and said, "God, have mercy on me, a sinner."   **Luke 18 v 13**

"I have a theory that selflessness and bravery aren't all that different."   Four, *Divergent*

When I first went to college, I bought a new car: an apple-red, '96 Chevy convertible LeBaron.

Before I left for school, my Dad told me: "Okay, Nick—just remember: every 4,000 miles, you need to change the oil. If you don't, all the money you saved on that car will be wasted." I fully intended to heed my Dad's instructions. I really did. It's just that, once I saw the price of an oil change, I decided to put it off.

My logic went something like this. I could either:

a) Buy an oil change now, OR

b) Buy 3,000 packs of Instant Noodles, and have a better chance than ANYONE of surviving the zombie apocalypse.

The choice was pretty obvious.

And as the months drew on, my decision to "wait" on the oil change was only confirmed. The car started making funny noises, and I ignored them. The oil light came on. I ignored it. Great deals on oil changes flew through my mailbox into the trash.

I started to think: "There's really no need for an oil change, is there? My LeBaron is special. She's an exception to the rule. She's invincible!" And then, two years to the day after I bought my brand new, shiny, red convertible, the transmission shut down.

Which meant: "Bye bye LeBaron."

Which also meant: "Bye bye car, for all of college."

Deceiving ourselves

A lot of times, to be honest, **I treat my relationship with God like I treated my Chevy LeBaron**. Even if I know something is wrong—actually, ESPECIALLY if I know something is wrong—I tend to ignore it. I don't dare lift the hood. I pretend that everything is fine. But deep down, I know: I have failures. Typically, I cope with that reality in one of two ways: "fix it" or "forget it."

Some of us try to fix our flaws through punishment: we binge, purge ourselves, or hide ourselves away from the world. We watch blood-splattered movies or cut ourselves to feel relieved: a price is paid. Blood is shed.

Others try to fix themselves through work: we're up past midnight making up for our last grade; we spend hours at the gym perfecting our flaws; or we come up with a program or list of rules to follow so we don't "mess up" next time.

Others just try to "forget it": we drink, do drugs, watch porn, spend money, or get lost in video games and movies. We distract ourselves from our failure with instant gratification.

We do it all, because it relieves us of our inner sense: that there's a price to be paid for failure. How do you pay the price? Here's an exercise: Finish this sentence: "When I mess up, I…"

1. _____

2. _____

3. _____

(If you have a hard time answering, think of this: "What do I do when I'm stressed?")

The tax collector

The tax collector isn't like most of us: He doesn't forget his shame. He doesn't fix his shame. He doesn't pray a long, elaborate prayer to make up for his flaws. He does the opposite:

> *But the tax collector stood at a distance. He would not even look up to heaven, but beat his breast and said, "God, have mercy on me, a sinner."* **Luke 18 v 13**

Can I share a secret with you?

I envy him.

I bet you do, too. I wish I didn't care what anyone thought. I wish I could stop "fixing it" or "forgetting it." I wish I felt free to be honest about my flaws—to stop being fake, forever.

But like the mouth of the tin man in *The Wizard of Oz*, **my mouth is stopped by the rust of my own shame**.

But the tax collector's mouth isn't—why?

Here's his secret. Are you ready? It's not accepting himself, warts and all. It's not looking in the mirror and saying: "I'm great!" It's the opposite. The tax collector says: "I'm not going to fix my flaws, or forget them." When he looks in the mirror, he says: "I give up."

The tax collector's secret

"So you're saying," you say, "that if I want to stop being a faker, I need to be completely hopeless?" Not quite. The tax collector gives up on himself, it's true. **But he doesn't give up on God.** In his prayer is a hidden secret... one of the most explosive truths you've ever heard.

When the tax collector says: "Have mercy on me, a sinner," he doesn't use the typical Greek word for "mercy." He uses a word used only a handful of times in the Bible. You've probably never heard it before. It's the word "propitiation."

"Propla-whoozee-whats-it!? Nick, you're being a nerd, again." Okay, yes—true. But stick with me for a moment. The word "propitiation" can change your life forever. Are you ready? Here's what it means...

When Adam and Eve lived in God's original temple—the Garden of Eden—the Bible tells us that God gave them a clear instruction:

> *"You must not eat from the tree of the knowledge of good and evil, for when you eat from it you will certainly die."*
>
> *Genesis 2 v 17*

Like in any kingdom, God the King and Judge told Adam and Eve that the price for their treason would be death.

So when God established his earthly temple—built in Jerusalem—he told the Israelites that they couldn't enter in, unless they died. But then, in another surprising move, God offered a way in: the priest

could bring death with him. Aaron would enter God's throne room covered in blood: the blood of a bull and a goat (Leviticus 16). Once a year, Aaron would take that blood, and paint it on God's throne—a visual reminder of what was required to stand before God, the King and Judge (Leviticus 16 v 14).

In other words, Aaron would substitute the blood of an animal for the life of God's people. And because of that **God's anger against his people was completely spent.** There wasn't one penny left: gone, nada, bye-bye, far away, on vacation to the moon.

That's propitiation—God takes the death we deserve, and places it on someone or something else. And in that way, we can come to God without shame… and without pride. That's how the tax collector is freed from his mask, forever: by propitiation.

A God of love?

Before we move on, let me address something. You might be surprised to hear that God requires death before we enter his temple. Because isn't it true, after all, that God is love?

PROPITIATION

Yes, it's true—God *is* love. But God's love isn't like our love. God's love overwhelms us and dethrones us. That's because it flows from his overwhelming beauty—his "holiness." When the Old Testament prophet Isaiah enters the temple, he sees three angels covering their eyes and feet with wings, shouting out:

> *Holy, holy, holy is the L*ORD *Almighty;*
> *the whole earth is full of his glory.*   *Isaiah 6 v 1-3*

Nowhere else in Scripture is a word repeated *three* times to describe God: God is "Holy, holy, holy." Which means: at his core, God is ridiculously, utterly, immeasurably holy. What is holiness? It's not just being pure—that's part of it. But **God isn't just pure: he's an overwhelming volcano of purity**. In fact, what holiness literally means is "separate." It's his above-ness and beyond-ness. God's holiness, as someone once put it, is God's "otherness."[1]

Some things about God make my brain feel like a microwaved creamsicle. He knows everything. He's present everywhere. He's always satisfied because of himself. He never changes. He has no beginning or end. He's three persons—Father, Son and Holy Spirit—but one God. When I try to put those things into words, my mouth is like a microwaved creamsicle. That's what it means that God is holy. He's completely, and utterly, indescribable. He's other.

So yes—God is love, mercy and compassion. But these are just some of the rays that shine off the sun of God's holiness. They're just some streams that flow forth from the volcano of his purity. There are others, too: justice, wrath, and an inability to dwell with sin.

So **to say "God is love" is true, but incomplete**. Love isn't god—God is, among other things, love. He isn't a god who loves like we do. His love is "other": it's better than our niceness. It flows from his volcanic, beautiful purity.

I love how Mr. Beaver refers to Aslan, the lion in C. S. Lewis's *The Lion, the Witch and the Wardrobe*:

> *"Safe?" said Mr. Beaver … "Who said anything about safe? 'Course he isn't safe. But he's good. He's the King, I tell you."*

If we want to be dethroned, we need to be overwhelmed. And we can only do that when we trade "nice/safe god" for the God who is *good*—the God who deserves to be King.

The tax collector's funeral

If there's one key difference between the Pharisee and the tax collector, it's this: **the tax collector, unlike the Pharisee, understands God's holiness**. He knows what's required to be in God's presence. Not a list of rules. Not "niceness." Not tolerance. But death.

And because of that, he beats his chest like an ancient Jew would have done at a funeral. He stands far away from the inner court, recognizing his unworthiness. And, most importantly, he uses this special word "propitiation." He says: *God, I know I'm a dead man without you—so please fix me through the blood of another.*

What an amazing, brilliant, astounding prayer!

And when he prayed it, Jesus says that something happened that turned his life around.

Chapter Six:
Unfreezing a frozen heart

I tell you that this man, rather than the other, went home justified before God.

Luke 18 v 14

"Only an act of true love can thaw a frozen heart."

Pabbie, Disney's *Frozen*

All throughout high school, I was convinced I was going to become a professional hockey player for the Detroit Red Wings. Why? Don't ask me (don't ask anyone who's seen me play hockey, either). I just knew it would happen.

I'd sit by our crackling, sputtering television every night during play-off season, trying to see through the fuzz my favorite players: Sergei Federov, Steve Yzerman, Darren McCarty. I knew one day I'd be on the ice with them.

I spent hours in 20-degrees-below-Fahrenheit (– 29° C) weather in the wee hours of the night, taking turns with my dad and brothers to spray a manufactured ice-rink in our backyard. I spent all of my summer savings on hockey camp. I even generously hooked my younger

brother up between hockey posts in our driveway so I could shoot a puck at him for hours on end.

He never did thank me.

There was only one flaw to my brilliant plan to become a pro: I wasn't any good. In fact, the first day I tried out, I barely made the hockey league, let alone a team. I'm pretty sure I was the only person who used my skates to *walk* through the cones that day. Then there was that moment I tripped and fell on my face near the popcorn stand.

So why did I believe I'd be a pro? I'll tell you why: I needed to believe. Being a Detroit Red Wing wasn't just about hockey: it was how I planned to *justify* myself.

Justifying ourselves

What does it mean to be justified? It means to be **officially declared good**. Now, listen closely, and I'll let you in on a secret: The need to be justified is what makes us *fakers* in the first place. "What?!" you say. "I've never even used the word *justified*." But think about it: everything we do is an attempt to be justified. We all want to be declared good, worthy of love, getting it right. Some of us try to justify ourselves by being great at sports, or getting good grades. Some of us try to work hard so we can make a lot of money, or so we can be attractive to the opposite sex. Some of us follow a list of religious rules.

We think: "When I have that, I'll be *good* (ie: justified)."

In fact, grab a pen or pencil and finish this sentence: "I will be good when…"

1. _____

2. _____

3. _____

Whatever you wrote down, *that is your god—the thing that will justify you.*

The Pharisee and the tax collector

The difference between the Pharisee and the tax collector was this: the Pharisee was trying to justify himself. He was using his god—religious rules—to win the approval of others. But the tax collector wasn't worried about being declared "good" by others—he sees that his true crisis was God's holiness vs. his sin. And he—the bad guy—was the one who went home justified by God.

That's what Jesus is showing us: if we want to stop being fakers, we need to stop trying to declare ourselves good. We need to put down our masks, and come humbly before God, the King and Judge of the universe.

Only he has the power to declare us good.

And here's the brilliant news—he does it in the most amazing way possible: through propitiation.

The problem with propitiation

Of course, that's a problem for us, isn't it? Because for one, I'm pretty sure you don't make it a habit to slaughter a goat every time you celebrate your birthday.

53

And the temple where this story takes place was destroyed 2,000 years ago.

So no temple = no propitiation.

Secondly, God makes clear in the Old and New Testaments that "it is impossible for the blood of bulls and goats to take away sins" (Hebrews 10 v 4). David says of God: "Sacrifice and offering you did not desire ... burnt offerings and sin offerings you did not require" (Psalm 40 v 6). Which means: the purpose of temple sacrifices *wasn't* to propitiate for sins. Rather, **it was to remind people that they needed propitiation for sin** (Hebrews 10 v 3).

This is what the tax collector knew.

But as Jesus' life progresses, we see a clearer picture emerging. A man named Paul, after Jesus' death and resurrection, uses the word "propitiation" to talk about Jesus himself: "God put [him] forward as a propitiation by his blood, to be received by faith" (Romans 3 v 25, ESV). When Jesus began his ministry near the River Jordan, a man named John saw him and said:

> *Look, the Lamb of God, who takes away the sin of the world!*
> *John 1 v 29*

Why a lamb? Because it reminds us of propitiation—an innocent lamb, slaughtered, to rescue God's people. John is saying: *Here's the propitiation for our sins—Jesus, God's Son.* Jesus says something similar, later in his ministry: "Whoever wants to be first must be your slave—just as the Son of Man did not come to be served, but to serve, and to give his life as a ransom for many" (Matthew 20 v 27-28).

Jesus is saying: *I am the sacrificial lamb of the temple. I am the propitiation for my people.* Jesus—God in the flesh—would be "led like a lamb to the slaughter" on the cross to take away our sins (Isaiah 53 v 7).

Why did God himself (in Jesus) need to become the lamb? *Because only God's infinite goodness can satisfy God's infinite holiness.*

Jesus is, in other words, *God himself taking away God's wrath.*

Creamsicle, right?

Frozen hearts

Toward the end of the movie *Frozen*, in a staggering, frozen daze, Princess Anna sees her evil sister Elsa's life in danger. Giving up her freedom from the magical freezing curse, Anna throws herself before the villain Hans's knife, and succumbs to the bitter cold. But as Elsa weeps over Anna's frozen body, something miraculous happens: she begins to melt. It's only then that the words of the wise troll Pabbie come to life: "Only true love can thaw a frozen heart."

The reason *Frozen* resonates with us, I believe, is this: God has written his love story on our hearts. We are frozen-hearted. We are loveless. We need an act of true love to rescue us. It's what we hear in all our favorite stories: Harry Potter faces the *Avada Kedavra* curse for his friends. Katniss gives up her life for her sister. Thor dies at the hand of the Destroyer for Jane.

And then, when we thought all hope was lost, they emerge victorious: there's resurrection.

These stories move our hearts because they point us to the true story of Christ: God in his incredible, mind-blowing love, *did* sacrifice himself for us. He came to be our high priest, who *also* offered himself up as our sacrificial lamb:

> *Surely he took up our pain and bore our suffering,*
> *yet we considered him punished by God,*
> *stricken by him, and afflicted.*
> *But he was pierced for our transgressions,*
> *he was crushed for our iniquities;*
> *the punishment that brought us peace was on him,*
> *and by his wounds we are healed.*
>
> *Isaiah 53 v 4-6*

And because of that, when we place our faith in Jesus, we too can be justified. Through the propitiation of Jesus' blood, we, like the tax collector, can be declared good. Jesus Christ defeated the death we deserve by dying in our place, and then by rising from the dead three days later. The victory is won. The battle is over. When we place our faith in him, we are united to his death and resurrection forever—because he died, we can live.

Now that is a mask-melting truth.

Our response

Every single one of us, the Bible says, has rebelled against God the King and Judge: "There is no one righteous, not even one; there is no one who understands; there is no one who seeks God. All have turned away, they have together become worthless; there is no one who does good, not even one" (Romans 3 v 10-12). And because of that, all of us have earned death (Hebrews 9 v 27).

But when we acknowledge God as King and Judge, we're free to see that **the God who is angry with us is also the God who takes our place**. And he does it in the most amazing way possible: "He ... did not spare his Son, but gave himself up for us all" (Romans 8 v 32).

I can't imagine giving up my son Caleb, or my son Owen, for you or anyone else. In fact, since having kids, I've found in myself something I never knew I had: a killer instinct. When cars go speeding by in the parking lot outside our apartment, I want to take a potato launcher and shoot through their window.

And yet the Bible says that **God, in his goodness, gave up a relationship more precious than anything you and I can imagine**. It was a relationship better than the best marriage. Better than the most googley-eyed date. Better than the best BFFs ever. It was a perfect, intimate relationship that existed forever, between a perfect Son and a perfect Father.

And they separated. Over us. Rebels. Because both of their hearts beat for rebels like you and me, they experienced the breaking of that perfect relationship. The Father was angry with the Son, and the Son suffered the anger of his Father—so that you and I never have to face that anger and separation. (If that makes you ask: "WHY in the world would they do that!?" I think you're starting to get how overwhelming this truth is.)

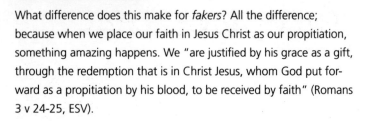

What difference does this make for *fakers*? All the difference; because when we place our faith in Jesus Christ as our propitiation, something amazing happens. We "are justified by his grace as a gift, through the redemption that is in Christ Jesus, whom God put forward as a propitiation by his blood, to be received by faith" (Romans 3 v 24-25, ESV).

Remember what *justification* means? It doesn't mean to be "tolerated" or even just "forgiven." It means **to be declared good**. Justification is God saying:

> BECAUSE OF JESUS, YOU ARE NOW, AND ALWAYS WILL BE, INFINITELY DELIGHTFUL TO ME. I'M AS CRAZY ABOUT YOU AS I AM ABOUT JESUS. I LIKE YOU. I DANCE OVER YOU. I SING OVER YOU. I WANT TO HEAR EVERY WORD YOU SAY — EVERY WHISPER. EVERYTHING JESUS HAS AS MY PERFECT SON, I GIVE TO YOU. YOU'RE PART OF THE FAMILY NOW. I ADOPT YOU, FOREVER.
>
> I WILL NEVER LET YOU GO.

And if the King and Judge of the universe says that about me, it doesn't really matter what other people think, does it?

It's just like Pabbie says: "Only an act of true love can thaw a frozen heart."

I think that's true of a frozen mask, too.

Chapter Seven:
God's love: real

Those who exalt themselves will be humbled, and those who humble themselves will be exalted.

Luke 18 v 14

"You love me. Real or not?"

Peeta, *The Hunger Games*

If you've never done so before, I want to invite you to place your faith in Jesus Christ right now. When you do that, all of the credit due to Jesus—who loved God and neighbor perfectly—is transferred to you. Not eventually. Not someday. Not after you perform a certain number of religious rituals: right now. The tax collector "went home" justified, without one good deed yet to his credit!

I'm praying now that one day in the new heaven and earth, we'll be telling your story, saying:

"And _____ walked away from that *Faker* book having placed their faith in Jesus. They were *justified*."

So, will you place your faith in Christ right now? You could even pray the same prayer as the tax collector: "God, have mercy on me, a sinner." The prayer isn't magic fairy-dust. It's just an expression of the fact that you have faith in God's promised Savior.

Will you trade your story of your own kingship for the story of God, the King, coming to earth for you?

Will you let go of your mask, and put on the robes of Christ (Romans 13 v 14), today? (If you don't know where to go from here, check the Epilogue on page 67 for some guidance.)

An eternal perspective

If you're not yet convinced, I want you to think about Jesus' last words in the parable: "Those who exalt themselves **will** be humbled, and those who humble themselves **will** be exalted."

When "will" they be? When God comes as returning King of the world.

Through Jesus' death, Jesus defeated death. But through his resurrection, he proved to be the King *who would raise the world to new life*. So although Jesus began his kingly reign here on earth 2,000 years ago, Jesus says one day he will come again to judge the nations: "At that time they will see the Son of Man (a title for Jesus) coming in a cloud with power and great glory" (Luke 21 v 27).

Which means—**if we reject King Jesus now, we will have no place in God's redeemed future world**. If we continue to wear our masks to exalt ourselves, we will be "humbled" on the day Jesus returns. And that day, unlike today, will last forever (Matthew 25 v 31-46).

But if we receive him in faith, Jesus says: "Those who humble themselves will be exalted" (Luke 18 v 14). As Jesus spreads his temple glory throughout the world, we will participate in the world as it is meant to be:

> *Look! God's dwelling place is now among the people, and he will dwell with them. They will be his people, and God himself will be with them and be their God. He will wipe every tear from their*

eyes. There will be no more death or mourning or crying or pain,
for the old order of things has passed away.

Revelation 21 v 3-4

And then we'll say, like Jewel the unicorn in C. S. Lewis's *The Last Battle*: "I have come home at last! This is my real country! I belong here. This is the land I have been looking for all my life, though I never knew it till now. The reason why we loved the old Narnia so much is because it sometimes looked a little like this."

We will belong to the home we've always looked for—the world as it is meant to be.

Justification now

Maybe you're saying: "Okay, Nick: I have placed my faith in Jesus. I see how that's supposed to melt my mask. But here's the thing: I still feel like a faker."

So let me be honest: I totally feel you.

I'm still a recovering fakeaholic. Just a couple of days ago, I made a big mistake and left my buddy waiting at the airport for me… when I wasn't there. I was a total wreck. For the next three nights, I woke up in a hot sweat. Whenever I saw a plane, my heart jumped out of my chest. I kept thinking: "Nick, you're such an idiot! How could you let that happen!?"

And while some people might say I had "low self-esteem," I know the truth: my self-esteem wasn't too low. It was too high. I didn't want my buddy to see my flaws. I wanted to keep up my mask. I still believed my justification before others was more important than God's justification through Jesus.

Even though my head believed the true story about Jesus, my heart wasn't believing it.

Maybe you feel the same way. Maybe you have faith in Christ, but you still find yourself slipping into bad habits with friends. Maybe you're still stressed about your flaws. Maybe you still try to "fix it" or "forget it" when you fail.

What do we do?

Swapping stories

I could give you lots of answers to this question, but the one I come back to is always the same: if we want to give up our masks, we need to swap stories. We need to forget the silly story about our fame, and soak ourselves in the true story of Jesus. Jesus, in this parable, calls us to "humble ourselves." The book of Isaiah shows us exactly what that means:

> *These are the ones I look on with favor:*
> *those who are humble and contrite in spirit,*
> *and who tremble at my word.*   *Isaiah 66 v 2*

God is saying: *If you want to forget your mask, you need soak in my word*. What is God's word? It's not a book of rules. It's the Bible—the magnificent story of God, the rightful King and Judge, climaxing in the person of Jesus Christ.

It's the story of God's **right** to reign.

It's the story of God **ruling** his people through the centuries.

It's the story of God's glorious **return**.

And most importantly, it's the story of **God's blazing holiness and jaw-gaping love in the person of his Son, King Jesus**. And when we soak in that story, we feel safe to forget our glory. Why? Because as we soak ourselves, we see four things, more and more clearly:

1. God is the rightful King and Judge of the universe.

2. We don't deserve kingship—we deserve death.

3. Jesus is our King and Judge, whose death and resurrection make those who trust in him infinitely delightful to himself.

4. Those with faith in Jesus' name will spend eternity reigning in his kingdom—the new earth.

Every single chapter of the Bible oozes with these four truths. And when we believe those truths, something amazing happens: we stop worrying about other people's opinions of us.

No more fretting

How does that work? Like this:

a) **When we soak in God's story, we don't need to fret about our failures.** Even if other people bug us about them, it doesn't matter. The King and Judge of the universe has already taken care of them: "Who will bring any charge against those whom God has chosen? It is God who justifies. Who then is the one who condemns? No one" (Romans 8 v 33-34).

b) **When we soak in God's story, we aren't able to "look down on" others.** The true story about Jesus tells us that we don't deserve honor or kingship: we deserve death. So we don't try to climb the social ladder. We don't daydream about ourselves. We don't even brag about ourselves: "For it is by grace you have been saved, through faith—and this is not from yourselves, it is the gift of God—not by works, so that no one can boast" (Ephesians 2 v 8-9).

When we trade our story for God's story, we also trade in our work for his work. We trade in our goodness for his goodness. We trade in our glory for his better, richer, holier glory. The true story about Jesus—the gospel—lets us finally breathe a sigh of relief. Through Jesus, **there's no more pressure to win the approval of anybody**. Not only that, but **the cycle of "looking down on others" and oppressing them is broken**. The story of the cross means justification for us and justice for the world.

It's truly amazing, isn't it? The gospel—the true story about Jesus—sets us free to be ourselves. We can rest in the fact that because of him, God has made us infinitely delightful to himself. Ever. Always. For all eternity. He won't let us go. So we can rest in his arms, every day, as we soak in his story. And from that inward change, we are set free to be just to others, in a world full of people who look down on one another.

Because as we receive the healing lotion of Jesus Christ, our masks—which tie us to our fears and force us to look down on others—slowly peel away like an ugly scab.

At the cross we see these two stunning realities about God: He is the holy King and Judge of our world. His overwhelming purity demands death for sin. He *dethrones* us.

But we also see something else: God's overwhelming love embraces us. It justifies us. It sets us free from proving ourselves through masks forever. I think of that famous question of Peeta to Katniss in Suzanne Collins' *Mockingjay*: "You love me. Real or not?" When I come to the story of King Jesus, I can safely ask: "God, you love me. Real or not?"

Because when I look at the cross, I see a resounding, jaw-dropping, mask-melting: **"Real."**

Epilogue:
Leaving Fakerville, forever

By now, some of you are wondering: "What do I do with all this?" You might feel a bit like we've taken a long train ride together, and I've just waved you off and said: "Good luck!" That's where this epilogue comes in. I can't give you a full tour of fake-free country, but I can give you a simple tool to help you soak in God's presence every day—to enjoy and appreciate your relationship with him. Think of it like the map that will guide the way. It's called: **prayer**.

VIP access

You'll notice the way in which Jesus takes the spiritual pulses of the Pharisee and the tax collector—he examines their prayer lives. How they speak to God tells us all we need to know about them. Like a spiritual x-ray, our prayer lives show us what's gone wrong inside. If you're experiencing *faker* symptoms, I guarantee your prayer life doesn't exist, or needs some serious spiritual resuscitation.

That being said, I realize prayer will be new to many of us. So, what is prayer? This is big: **prayer is entering the throneroom of God's temple**. Before Jesus' death and resurrection, if you wanted to go to where God dwelled, you needed to go to the temple, just like the Pharisee and the tax collector did. But now, God dwells in his people—his Spirit lives in the heart of anyone and everyone who has placed their faith in Jesus (Ephesians 1 v 13-14; 1 Corinthians 3 v 16). God's temple is no longer a place; it's a people.

Now stop a moment, and think about that. **The God of the universe— the King and Judge of creation—has chosen to make his home in your heart.** Because you are God's temple, you have VIP access to the most dangerous, and beautiful, place that exists: the Most Holy Place—God's throneroom.

When I was younger, once a year my dad would take me to his work in an air-traffic control tower. The security guards let me through. People gave me high fives. I was let into the most magical place a kid could imagine: the radar room, with its beeping, blinking lights, and glow-in-the-dark keypads. It was a place where no kid was ever allowed to go, except for me: because my dad worked there.

When we go to prayer, we're experiencing the same thing; because of Jesus, we are, spiritually speaking, walking into the greatest place possible. We get to play in God's throneroom, because he is our dad.

The faker's prayer

In our parable, we saw two examples of prayer: a horrible one, and a good one. The difference between them gives us an important prayer principle: **prayer isn't about impressing God**. When we pray, it's not like we're "trying out for the team." Through Jesus,

we made the team! We can boldly go to God, without having to put on a show. Because of Jesus, we can be real. Prayer isn't about showing off our story to God—it's about freely soaking in his.

So, what does this look like? Fortunately, Jesus' disciples asked the same question. This is how Jesus responded:

When you pray, say:

"Father,
hallowed be your name,
your kingdom come.
Give us each day our daily bread.
Forgive us our sins,
for we also forgive everyone who sins against us.
And lead us not into temptation."

Luke 11 v 2-4

Each of these phrases was carefully chosen by Jesus to show us each corner of God's throneroom. Let's explore them one by one:

"Father"

Jesus wants us to begin prayer by remembering our relationship to God: God is our Father. When you start praying, start by remembering your new relationship to God. Say something like: "God, I know that because of Jesus, you have adopted me as your son/daughter. I believe you're listening to every word I say, and you're here with me, right now." This will electrify the rest of the conversation.

"Hallowed be your name"

When Jesus says "hallowed," he's not talking about trick-or-treating. He's talking about God's holiness. He's saying to God the Father: "I want your name to be set apart." This second part of prayer is crucial for *fakers*. You know from this book that God is King. And Judge. And holy. But taking time to praise God helps us soak in those truths. It's like the difference between reading a movie synopsis and sitting down to watch the movie.

For this, and every other step, it's very important you begin by reading the Bible. **Trying to pray without the Bible is like trying to light a fire without wood.** The Bible gives us the substance we need to pray. So use a Bible-reading plan (the "Engage" series from The Good Book Company website is the best place to start, see page 78), and ask yourself: "What did my Bible reading teach me about God today?" Write it down, if that helps. Then tell God how his character and work delight you.

"Your kingdom come"

In our chapter about the temple, we talked about God's *right* to be King, his *reign* as King, and his *return* as King. This is what Jesus is praying for here. He's praying for God's kingdom to be realized. What does this look like? The easiest answer to that question is this: it's a world where we live according to God's word. For this second part of the prayer, ask yourself: "What did my Bible reading teach me about what God wants today?" Write it down. Now you're ready to respond in three ways:

"Give us each day our daily bread"

God's call to live as someone who belongs to his kingdom will sometimes make you squirm. You'll think: "But what will SHE say?" or: "But how can I do that and still do well in school?" or: "People will rip me apart for this!" That's why Jesus makes the next part of the prayer: "Give us each day our daily bread." It's a reminder that God will take care of all our needs, no matter what, so we can fearlessly put God's priorities and his kingdom first. So, what's making you anxious? What's distracting you in prayer? Tell all of these things to God, as honestly as you can.

"Forgive us our sins, for we also forgive everyone who sins against us"

Now it's time to get real. As with the tax collector in our story, seeing who God is, and what his kingdom demands, will overwhelm us.

But because of Jesus, we can boldly come before God and confess our failure: "God, I really messed up. Please forgive me, because of Jesus." The habit of confessing our failures and assuring ourselves of the truth about what Jesus has done for us may just be the #1 way to overcome our *faker* tendencies.

(PS—the second part about forgiving everyone else is Jesus' gentle reminder of how his forgiveness should transform our behavior, and that's not an "I'll forgive others so God will forgive me" attitude!)

"And lead us not into temptation"

Now take the truths you learned about God's character and his kingdom, and imagine if they were radically lived out in your life. Boldly ask God that his Spirit will empower you to do just that (see Ephesians 3 v 14-21). Pray the same for others. Jesus promises that when we ask for this, he will answer in powerful ways: "So I say to you: Ask and it will be given to you; seek and you will find; knock and the door will be opened to you" (Luke 11 v 9). Isn't that incredible? Why would he do such a thing?

There's only one answer to that question: it's because of Jesus. Remember, **if you're justified, when God looks at you, he sees his Son. When you speak, he hears his Son.** He isn't folding his arms, checking his phone. It's as if you're the only person in the world speaking to him.

My prayer for you

I promise you, if you take 15 to 30 minutes every day to pray like this, you'll start to experience the change we've talked about in this book. I've seen it in my own life. As I've come to God in prayer, and soaked in his story, he has made himself real to me. I've seen my mask melting. I've heard the noise of the crowds fade quietly into the background.

I pray this book will be one small step in that direction for you. I pray that your fearless, mask-less life will cause others to wonder. I pray that you will step boldly into God's presence. I pray that you will get real with others, and be free of the faker roller coaster forever.

In a word: I pray that you will lift Jesus up, and change the world, *for real*.

Endnotes

Chapter Two

1. NY Daily News, "Lady Gaga Interviewed by Elton John for V Magazine: My Fans are 'My Medicine, My Religion.'" May 13, 2011

Chapter Three

1. G.K. Beale's insights in "The Temple and the Church's Mission" have been indispensable for me in creating this section.

Chapter Four

1. Kohlenberger III, "Expanded Vine's Expository Dictionary of New Testament Words", p. 571-572

Chapter Five

1. Kohlenberger III, as above, p. 37

Nicholas T. McDonald has been a student pastor for seven years, and was educated at Olivet Nazarene University, Oxford University, and Gordon Conwell Theological Seminary (M.Div). He and his wife, Brenna, love to travel and speak to students. You can check out Nicholas's work at his blog, *www.scribblepreach.com*, where he writes on faith, culture, and ministry.

Prayer chart

You may want to write or draw your prayers. This chart will help you do this. The six pics on the right are easy to remember and draw, as you take each part of Jesus' prayer and pray it through for yourself. You can also download this from **www.thegoodbook.com/faker**

1. Father	Remind yourself of your position before God. You are his adopted child, and he is listening, like a loving Father, to everything you say.	
2. Hallowed be your name	Think of how the Bible passage you're reading tells you about God's character. Tell God how awed you are at who he is.	
3. Your kingdom come	Reflect on what the passage you're reading tells you about what God wants. How does he want us to live as those who belong to his kingdom?	
4. Give us each day our daily bread	How does the Bible passage you're reading calm your anxieties? How does it demonstrate that God will provide for all your needs, especially through Jesus?	
5. Forgive us our sins	Think of ways in which you've failed to respond to God's character, live as a member of his kingdom, and trust in his provision throughout the day. Bring those confessions to Jesus, and take time to remember—you've been forgiven and justified, because of him.	
6. Lead us not into temptation	Pray that today, you can put God's priorities and his kingdom first, especially in places where you've failed. Pray the same prayer for your family, and friends. Pray for anyone else who comes to mind.	

LOST

A son turns his back on home and family to follow his dreams of a new life on his own. Another son stays dutifully at home.

But **when the dream turns to a nightmare**, what will this first son do? And which of the two sons is really the more lost?

In this deceptively simple story, Jesus gets to the heart of what it means to be lost to God, and found by him again. And it's a story that's **full of surprises**.

You'll be surprised by the father, surprised by the sons, and surprised by what this story tells us about our own hearts.

And that's the biggest surprise of all...

Jaw-dropping in fact...

FEARLESS

Turn upside down everything you knew about bravery as God helps Daniel and his mates to stand firm under pressure.

HERO

Turn upside down everything you knew about fame and significance as God transforms Gideon into the unlikeliest of heroes.

Available from all good retailers or direct from:

North America: www.thegoodbook.com
UK: www.thegoodbook.co.uk
Australia: www.thegoodbook.com.au
New Zealand: www.thegoodbook.co.nz

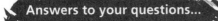

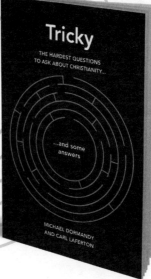

thegoodbook
COMPANY

Opening up the Bible

At The Good Book Company, we are dedicated to helping Christians and local churches grow. We believe that God's growth process always starts with hearing clearly what he has said to us through his timeless word—the Bible.

Ever since we opened our doors in 1991, we have been striving to produce resources that honor God in the way the Bible is used. We have grown to become an international provider of user-friendly resources to the Christian community, with believers of all backgrounds and denominations using our Bible studies, books, evangelistic resources, DVD-based courses and training events.

We want to equip ordinary Christians to live for Christ day by day, and churches to grow in their knowledge of God, their love for one another, and the effectiveness of their outreach.

Call us for a discussion of your needs or visit one of our local websites for more information on the resources and services we provide.

North America: www.thegoodbook.com
UK & Europe: www.thegoodbook.co.uk
Australia: www.thegoodbook.com.au
New Zealand: www.thegoodbook.co.nz

North America: 866 244 2165
UK & Europe: 0333 123 0880
Australia: (02) 6100 4211
New Zealand (+64) 3 343 1990

www.christianityexplored.org

Our partner site is a great place for those exploring the Christian faith, with a clear explanation of the good news, powerful testimonies and answers to difficult questions.

One life. What's it all about?